THE OFFICIAL CELTIC ANNUAL 2022

THE CELTIC FOOTBALL CLUB 1888

Written by Joe Sullivan
Designed by Chris Dalrymple

A Grange Publication

CONTENTS

ROLL OF HONOUR

Scottish League Winners [51 times]
1892/93, 1893/94, 1895/96, 1897/98,
1904/05, 1905/06, 1906/07, 1907/08,
1908/09, 1909/10, 1913/14, 1914/15,
1915/16, 1916/17, 1918/19, 1921/22,
1925/26, 1935/36, 1937/38, 1953/54,
1965/66, 1966/67, 1967/68, 1968/69,
1969/70, 1970/71, 1971/72, 1972/73,
1973/74, 1976/77, 1978/79, 1980/81,
1981/82, 1985/86, 1987/88, 1997/98,
2000/01, 2001/02, 2003/04, 2005/06,
2006/07, 2007/08, 2011/12, 2012/13,
2013/14, 2014/15, 2015/16, 2016/17,
2017/18, 2018/19, 2019/20

Scottish Cup Winners [40 times]
1892, 1899, 1900, 1904, 1907, 1908,
1911, 1912, 1914, 1923, 1925, 1927,
1931, 1933, 1937, 1951, 1954, 1965,
1967, 1969, 1971, 1972, 1974, 1975,
1977, 1980, 1985, 1988, 1989, 1995,
2001, 2004, 2005, 2007, 2011, 2013,
2017, 2018, 2019, 2020

League Cup Winners [19 times]
1956/57, 1957/58, 1965/66, 1966/67,
1967/68, 1968/69, 1969/70, 1974/75,
1982/83, 1997/98, 1999/00, 2000/01,
2005/06, 2008/09, 2014/15, 2016/17,
2017/18, 2018/19, 2019/20

European Cup Winners 1967
Coronation Cup Winners 1953

ANGE POSTECOGLOU

BACK in June, it was announced that Ange Postecoglou had been appointed manager of Celtic Football Club after a successful spell in Japan with J1 League outfit, Yokohama F Marinos, where he led them to the title.

Both Ange's playing and managerial careers started with Melbourne South, and the Greek-born Australian is the only man to have been involved in all four of the Lakeside Stadium side's NSL title-winning teams – the first two as player and the second two as manager.

Winning silverware has become something of a habit for the 56-year-old. As well as winning national titles as manager with Hellas and Marinos, he has also done likewise with Brisbane Roar.

Added to that, while overseeing the Australian national youth set-up, he managed Under-17, U19 and U20 levels to international championship wins in both the Oceana and Asian federations before leading the Australian senior side to glory in the AFC Asian Cup to add to the Aussie caps he won at Under-20 and senior levels as a player.

When Ange lifted the Asian Cup in 2015, it was the first time the Aussies had ever won this title. Ange also managed the Australian national team at the FIFA World Cup in 2014 in Brazil and led Australia to qualification in 2018 in Russia.

He has also received a host of prestigious personal coaching accolades, including being named as Australia's PFA Manager of the Decade in 2015, and even though he looked set for a very successful career in Japan with Yokohama F Marinos, when the call came from Celtic he just couldn't say no to the club.

MANAGER FACTFILE

Angelos Postecoglou
D.O.B: 27/08/65
Born: Nea Filadelfeia, Athens, Greece

Playing career record:
South Melbourne (1984-1993),
Western Suburbs (1994).

Playing honours:
South Melbourne: National Soccer League
Championship (1984, 1990/91) National
Soccer League Premiership (1992/93),
National Soccer League Southern
Conference (1984, 1985), NSL Cup
(1989/90).

As Manager:

South Melbourne:
NSL Premiership (1997/98), NSL
Championship (1997/98, 1998/99),
Oceana Club Championship (1999).

Brisbane Roar:
A-League Premiership (2010/11),
A-League Championship (2010/11,
2011/12).

Australia:
AFC Asian Cup (2015).

Yokohama F Marinos:
J1 League (2019).

FORREST FLASHBACK
FILES No.1 JAMES FORREST'S LIFE AS A CELT

JAMES Forrest is now Celtic's longest-serving player with over 400 appearances since making his debut in 2010 as an 18-year-old.

Your 2022 Celtic Annual has dipped into the vaults for the Forrest Flashback Files to find out what makes, or made, him Tic'.

Here, we travel back over a decade as the midfielder was under the spotlight answering questions on That's Entertainment and Cinema Paradiso features.

JAMES FORREST

Are you a regular cinema goer?
No, probably just about once a month. I prefer watching a DVD.

What is your snack of choice at the pictures?
I always have toffee popcorn.

Greatest film you have seen at the cinema?
The Hangover - it was just really funny and I really enjoyed it. I prefer going to see comedy films.

Worst film you have seen at the cinema?
The Men Who Stare at Goats – it was out last year and it was the worst film I have ever seen in my life. It was going nowhere. Everything about it was bad.

Who is your favourite actor/actress?
Johnny Depp. He was really good in Pirates of the Caribbean. I've modelled my life on Jack Sparrow!

James Forrest

What's your favourite piece of music on your iPod?

Some stuff by U2

Who is your favourite group/artist of all time?

U2 again.

What was the best gig you have ever been to?

T in the Park. I also went to see Akon he was pretty good.

What is your favourite film?

Law Abiding Citizen was one of the films I saw last season and it was really good.

What TV programme do you never miss?

Friends, I have always watched it growing up.

SEASON

JULY

FRANCE was the destination for Celtic in the summer as teams all over the continent prepared to start the season in front of very few supporters - or no fans at all.

The Hoops played some formidable foes during their short trip across the channel as they faced up to OGC Nice, Olympique Lyonnais and Paris Saint-Germain over the course of just five days in the summer heat.

First up were Nice at the Groupama Stadium in Lyon and the Hoops came from behind to draw 1-1, thanks to a goal from Patryk Klimala in the 73rd minute after the French side had gone ahead through Kasper Dolberg in the 38th minute.

REVIEW

Just two days later at the same venue, former Celt, Moussa Dembele opened the scoring for Lyon before Memphis Depay added another before half time. Mohammed Elyounoussi pulled one back three minutes from time, but it was too little too late.

The third and final game always looked the toughest test on paper, and that's exactly how it turned out to be as a high-flying PSG scored twice either side of the break for a 4-0 scoreline.

SEASON

AUGUST

THE season got underway in earnest at the start of August, and the first Sunday of the month saw the title flag unfurled at Paradise under eerily quiet circumstances with no fans in the ground due to the Covid-19 lockdown.

Flag Day on the pitch carried on as normal, though, with an Odsonne Edouard goal paving the way for an opening-day 5-1 win to start the campaign off with three points.

However, the following week saw a penalty give Kilmarnock a share of the points at Rugby Park. Celtic's scheduled games against St Mirren and Aberdeen were postponed due to Covid-19.

Further SPFL action and European competition took up the rest of the month with the full six points being delivered on the domestic front with a 1-0 win over Dundee United at Tannadice followed by a fine 3-0 win over Motherwell at Celtic Park.

REVIEW

There were, however, differing fortunes in the Champions League qualifiers which had been trimmed to one-off games thanks to the grip of Coronavirus, and an enjoyable 6-0 win over Icelandic side KR Reykjavik was followed by another home game, this time against Ferencvaros of Hungary.

The tight 2-1 scoreline in favour of the Budapest side saw the Hoops parachute into the Europa League qualifying rounds.

SEPTEMBER

THERE were five straight wins during the month of September, with one Europa League victory amid 12 points from 12 in the four SPFL meetings.

New signing, Shane Duffy got off to a flier by scoring in his first two appearances as the Celts travelled to Ross County and then St Mirren with a result of 5-0 in the Highlands followed by a 2-1 win in Paisley.

Livingston were next on the agenda at Celtic Park and, after the visitors opened the scoring from the spot, the Hoops sped to a 3-1 lead before the West Lothian side pulled it back to 3-2 just 12 minutes from time to make for a nervy ending to the game.

Then followed a potentially precarious trip to Latvia to take on Riga in a one-off Europa League tie and, just when it looked like going to extra-time, Mohammed Elyounoussi struck to give Celtic the 1-0 win.

The month was rounded off with the visit of Hibernian to Celtic Park, and goals in the seventh, 35th and 79th minutes from Callum McGregor, Albian Ajeti and Elyounoussi eased Celtic to a 3-0 win.

OCTOBER

JUST a week after beating Riga in the Europa League qualifier, Celtic faced a tougher assignment in Bosnia when they met FK Sarajevo, but a dominant display marked by a goal from Odsonne Edouard put the Celts into the group-stage draw.

The draw in Nyon saw the Celts go into a tough Group H alongside AC Milan, Sparta Prague and Lille, with two of those games scheduled before the end of the month.

In Celtic's group opener, a 2-0 deficit was pulled back to 2-1 when Mohamed Elyounoussi scored with 14 minutes left.

However, a last-minute goal gave Milan a 3-1 win, and in the next game in France, a 2-0 lead from an Elyounoussi double was pulled back to 2-2 by Lille.

On the domestic front, two goals at the end of the 90 minutes gave the Hoops a 2-0 win at St Johnstone when a 0-0 draw looked on the cards, but there was defeat in the SPFL match when Rangers visited.

Celtic's final SPFL match of the month saw a trip to Pittodrie, and Aberdeen opening and closing the scoring with penalties – the last spot-kick securing a 3-3 draw for the home side.

NOVEMBER

CELTIC had just played Aberdeen the previous Sunday and this time the teams clashed in the re-arranged Covid-hit Scottish Cup semi-final of the previous season.

This time the proceedings weren't as dramatic as the 3-3 Pittodrie draw, as goals from Ryan Christie and Mohamed Elyounoussi in the first half paved the way to a final against Hearts and the aim of the Quadruple Treble was still on.

Things weren't so glossy in Europe, though, as two 4-1 defeats to Sparta Prague dented the hopes of progress from Group H.

REVIEW

Back on the league front, a sterling 4-1 win over Motherwell at Fir Park featuring a Mo Elyounoussi hat-trick was followed by another away trip, this time to Easter Road where a last-minute goal from new Bhoy, Diego Laxalt could only earn Celtic a 2-2 draw.

While the first game of the month kept Celtic on the road to a possible Quadruple Treble, the final game killed any hopes of continuing that run into season 2020/21 as a 2-0 win for Ross County in the League Cup was Celtic's first domestic cup defeat in 36 games.

DECEMBER

As the final game of November showed, the magnificent winning run in cup competitions, and consecutive trophies won had to end somewhere – but would December deliver the seemingly improbable Quadruple Treble?

That was the big question at the start of the final month of the year, but we all now know the answer as the bizarreness of the 2019/20 Scottish Cup final played in the 2020/21 season just a few days before Christmas in front of no supporters proved to be another Hampden high for the Hoops.

A Europa League group match saw a 4-2 defeat in Milan followed by an unwelcome 1-1 draw with St Johnstone in the league at Celtic Park. However, that was followed by a final 3-2 win over Lille in the Europa League and a 2-0 defeat of Kilmarnock prior to the game that was on everyone's minds.

Hearts stood between Celtic and footballing history and it proved to be a game in which the ascendancy swung to and fro. Celtic's 2-0 lead was pulled back and the 90 minutes finished 2-2 before another half-hour of football saw each side score again.

The 3-3 stalemate went to spot kicks with young keeper, Conor Hazard providing heroics by saving two penalties, and it was Kristoffer Ajer who slotted away the defining penalty in the 4-3 shoot-out win.

So that was it, the Quadruple Treble, 12 consecutive trophies and a history-making fourth successive Scottish Cup win ensured a very Merry Christmas for the Celtic Family.

The rest of the festive season delivered three more SPFL wins in the shape of a 2-0 victory over Ross County at home, a 3-0 win at Hamilton Accies and another 3-0 result over Dundee United back at Paradise.

JANUARY

THE first month of the new calendar year was a busy one on the football front for the Hoops with no fewer than six SPFL games on the cards.

However, success was hard to come by in these games with two defeats sandwiching three draws and a solitary win. The month started as a 10-man Celtic were left disappointed by a 1-0 defeat to Rangers at Ibrox, with the home side scoring nine minutes after Nir Bitton's straight red card dismissal just over the hour mark.

January's final game also saw a reverse as St Mirren visited Celtic Park and, despite the Hoops pulling level via Odsonne Edouard, first-half goals either side of the Frenchman's strike saw the Saints return to Paisley with all three points.

REVIEW

In between times, Celtic were held to a 1-1 home draw with Hibernian as a late Kevin Nisbet goal cancelled out a superb David Turnbull free-kick which had given the Hoops the lead with nine minutes of the match remaining.

That was followed by a double-header against a high-flying Livingston side on the back of a nine-game winning run. The first game at Celtic Park finished 0-0 before a 2-2 draw four days later in Livingston amid difficult weather conditions for both sides.

Moi Elyounoussi and Bitton gave Celtic a first-half lead after the home side had opened the scoring, but Livingston equalised just before the hour mark, and the Hoops ended the game with 10 men after Scott Brown was sent off.

The sole win came at Paradise in a midweek game as goals from Leigh Griffiths and Edouard gave the Hoops a 2-0 win over Hamilton Accies.

FEBRUARY

THE month of February was even busier than January with seven SPFL games on the schedule, and although it was ultimately more successful with six wins and only one defeat – that single loss was to play the most significant role.

For the opener, Celtic put four past Kilmarnock without reply at Rugby Park. After dominating possession in the opening stages, Scott Brown fired his side in front ahead of the half-hour mark from a David Turnbull corner, before Odsonne Edouard bagged a brace in the second period, and Albian Ajeti got on the scoresheet in the final five minutes.

A few days later, Celtic welcomed Motherwell as young Stephen Welsh scored his first goal for the Hoops and Edouard added another before the visitors pulled one back in a 2-1 win for the Celts.

REVIEW

Celtic then produced another strong away performance, replicating the 4-0 result they recorded the previous week against Kilmarnock to see off St Mirren in Paisley as Tom Rogic scored the opener after 15 minutes. In a dominant second half, a flurry of goals from Edouard, Ryan Christie and David Turnbull within the space of five minutes gave the side a comfortable and well-deserved victory.

Next up was a visit to McDiarmid Park where Edouard was the hero as a dramatic quarter-hour of football saw St Johnstone take the lead soon after the break, only for the Frenchman to score two goals inside less than three minutes to reverse the lead for a 2-1 Hoops win.

The month also featured two 1-0 wins over Aberdeen at Celtic Park, the first of those featuring a wonder goal from Turnbull, while Edouard came up with the goods in the second game.

Those wins over the Dons, however, sandwiched a trip to Dingwall to take on Ross County, where a 70th-minute header from Jordan White was enough to give the home side the win, and manager, Neil Lennon parted company with Celtic in the aftermath of the defeat.

MARCH

FOLLOWING the flurry of games in January and February, the month of March saw little in the way of action for Celtic with international duty requiring the attention of many of the Hoops players in the latter stages of the month.

In the case of the Scotland Bhoys, this meant World Cup qualifying matches against Austria, Israel and Faroe Islands, with the Hoops limited to only two matches during March.

John Kennedy, having taken over as interim manager, got off to a winning start the previous month with his first game in charge being the 1-0 win over Aberdeen in February's final game.

However, he had to settle for a share of the spoils in his next two matches as his side were held to a goal-less draw with Dundee United at Tannadice.

The Hoops, though, were unfortunate not to have come away with a win over United, having dominated possession and created plenty of chances in front of goal throughout the 90 minutes.

There was a similar outcome in the next game at Celtic Park as the Hoops were held to a draw by Rangers following a dominant Glasgow derby display.

The home side fired themselves in front in the 23rd minute, when Odsonne Edouard showed great footwork and force down the left flank to cross for Mohamed Elyounoussi in the box. After losing his man, the Norwegian threw himself at the ball with an unstoppable diving header past the keeper.

Just four minutes after that, Celtic were denied a strong penalty claim. After some wonderful close control by Elyounoussi, the ball found Edouard and he appeared to be fouled. Referee, Willie Collum instead booked the Frenchman for simulation, despite replay footage showing clear contact. The visitors equalised in the 38th minute and the game finished 1-1.

APRIL

COME April, Scottish Cup business was back on the agenda for Celtic as the month would see two games in the competition alongside another two SPFL meetings.

The Hoops booked their place in the fourth round of the Scottish Cup with a dominant 3-0 win over Falkirk at Paradise. John Kennedy's side completely controlled the game from start to finish and were unfortunate not to have scored more goals with the chances they created.

James Forrest opened the scoring early in the second half in his first start in almost seven months. Ryan Christie quickly followed up to double Celtic's lead and Mohamed Elyounoussi rounded off the scoring with a lovely finish 10 minutes from the end.

More Premiership action was next as Livingston visited Celtic Park and the Hoops produced a dazzling 6-0 win over the West Lothian side.

REVIEW

James Forrest made it two for two when he broke the deadlock on the half-hour mark, before David Turnbull converted a Moi Elyounoussi cross to double the Hoops' lead before the break.

An own goal from the visitors five minutes into the second period set the tone for the remainder of the afternoon, before two sublime strikes from Elyounoussi and a fine Christie goal minutes from time rounded off a devastating display.

Next up was more Scottish Cup action and it was a disappointing afternoon at Ibrox for Celtic as the holders lost 2-0 to their city rivals. Both goals came in the first half, and though the Hoops created numerous chances, including a penalty with 10 minutes remaining, they were unable to convert any of them.

April finished off with the long trip to Pittodrie, and the home side took the lead in the 17th minute, and that was the way it stood until Leigh Griffiths helped Celtic salvage a draw with a goal in the final seconds of the game.

It took Celtic until the 93rd minute to put away one of the many chances created with Griffiths' header securing a point for the Hoops.

MAY

THERE were only three games in the final month of the 2020/21 season, and while the first was a damp squib, the final two games of the year were about one man – Scott Brown.

The opening game saw a trip to Ibrox, and although Odsonne Edouard equalised three minutes after the home side's opener, Rangers scored again before the break and did likewise after the turnaround before finding the net again in time added on.

It was 10 days before the Hoops played again and it was a midweek game against a St Johnstone side who would soon add the Scottish Cup to the League Cup won earlier in the season for their own double after four seasons of Celtic Trebles.

From a Celtic point of view, though, it was all about the man who had lifted all 12 of those trophies in the Quadruple Treble as well as nine-in-a-row amid a clutch of other trophy wins – this would be Scott Brown's last game for the Hoops at Paradise.

And his team-mates turned up with the goods as they swept the Perthshire side away with a 4-0 win for their captain.

Two goals in as many minutes from David Turnbull and Odsonne Edouard capped some confident possession play in the opening stages, before the Celts turned the screw in the second period with strikes from Kris Ajer and Karamoko Dembele who grabbed his own ray of the limelight on the night with his first goal for the Hoops.

Brown's very last game was still to come, though, and it was fitting that Easter Road was the venue – that was also where he played his very last game for Hibernian in 2007 when they beat Celtic 2-1 and both sets of fans cheered his goal in the game prior to him joining the Hoops.

Crowd or no crowd, though, there would be no goal celebrations of any kind in this match as both sides failed to find the net, although Celtic dominated the game and could have been three goals ahead at half-time, but Hibs sat deep and managed to prevent the Hoops from taking the win their play merited.

As a sign of the respect in which he is still held at Easter Road, Broony was presented with an inscribed silver salver by Hibs captain, David Gray, before the game.

At the end of the game he was embraced by Lewis Stevenson, who not only is Hibernian's longest-serving player, but he also played alongside Broony in that Easter Road match in 2007.

FORREST FLASHBACK FILES No.2
JAMES FORREST'S LIFE AS A CELT

The Official CELTIC Annual 2013

1888-2013

JAMES Forrest featured on the Celtic Annual cover for the first time in 2013 and that same issue saw him recall his first appearance on the hallowed Paradise turf in our *Home Bhoys* feature.

...tic Soccer
...s School

...e trade from the best in the business.

– JAMES FORREST

...citing in football than watching a wide-
... havoc on an opposition defence.

When the route to goal is congested, they can provide a moment of magic to conjure up a chance for others or themselves, whether through a piece of skill, a dangerous delivery or a burst of speed.

Celtic fans have always held a special affection for these types of players – the likes of Jimmy Johnstone, Charlie Tully and Bobby Lennox were all firm favourites in Paradise.

The latest wing wizard to grace the Hoops is Youth Academy graduate, James Forrest, who has proven his ability on the big stage for club and country since breaking into the first team.

Here are his top skills to learn to become successful in this important position.

Crossing the ball

If you have the time, have a look up and see who is in the box. If you aren't able to do that, just try and hit a good area in the box and hopefully one of the strikers can get on the end of it. You can either stand it up to the back post or try and whip it in to the near post and then hopefully someone in the box can finish it off.

The following year, the midfielder popped up in our Celtic Soccer Skills School when he let young aspiring footballers into the tricks of the trade in playing on the wing.

Using speed to good effect

I am fast, but there are a lot of defenders that can handle quicker players, so you need to be a wee bit cleverer than just simply knocking the ball past them and running on to it.

Skills in a one-on-one situation

Some people like using step-overs and some people prefer not to. It just depends on what skill you feel comfortable with. I sometimes use a step-over, as that can be a good way to catch a defender off balance. It just depends how the game is going and who you are playing against as everyone is different.

Using movement to find space

You always need to keep on your toes. By running forward five yards and then checking back you can get some space and try and get the ball that way. Movement is a big thing for wingers and it's all about getting on the ball.

Remember to work hard when you don't have the ball

The defensive side of the game is also important. You are part of a team, so it's not always just about attacking and taking players on but about doing your bit when the opposition has the ball. As a winger, this means covering your full-back to help them out and also tucking inside into midfield when required as well.

Advice for a budding footballer

Just remember to go and express yourself if you are a forward-thinking player. Feel confident in your ability and what you are doing. And, of course, it's important to work hard to develop your game as well.

JAMES FORREST

I HAD been in the squad for a while because I had spent most of the season training with them. Tony Mowbray had put me on the bench about six or seven times before I actually got to come on as a sub for my debut. It was kind of frustrating in a way to have been so close so many times so it was really good when I finally got to come on.

Neil Lennon told me when he got the job, about a month before that, that he wanted to give me my chance. He said he was going to wait for a game we were two or three nil up before he tried to put me on. It was 2-0 when I got on but then I scored and so did Robbie Keane, right at the end, and that made it 4-0.

I suppose I was nervous before it but once you're on the park it feels alright. It was okay warming up because I had already done that a few times when I was on the bench, but it was when it came to running on, I was a bit nervous then. I was fine when I got into it, though.

PARADISE

CALLUM McGREGOR

Position: Midfielder   **Squad Number:** 42
D.O.B: 14/06/93   **Born:** Glasgow, Scotland
Height: 5'10"   **Signed:** 07/07/09
Debut: v KR Reykjavik (a) 1-0, (UCL) 15/07/14
Previous Clubs: Celtic Youth (on loan at Notts County while with Celtic)

JAMES FORREST

Position: Winger   **Squad Number:** 49
D.O.B: 07/07/91   **Born:** Prestwick, Scotland
Height: 5'9"   **Signed:** 01/07/09
Debut: v Motherwell (h) 4-0, (SPL) 01/05/10
Previous Clubs: Celtic Youth

VASILIS BARKAS

Position: Goalkeeper   **Squad Number:** 1
D.O.B: 30/05/94   **Born:** Zetten, Netherlands
Height: 6'4"   **Signed:** 30/08/20
Debut: v Kilmarnock (a) 1-1, (SPFL) 09/08/20
Previous Clubs: AEK Athens, Atromitos

TOM ROGIC

Position: Midfielder   **Squad Number:** 18
D.O.B: 16/12/92   **Born:** Griffith, Australia
Height: 6'2"   **Signed:** 09/01/13
Debut: v Inverness Caley Thistle (a) 3-1, (SPL) 09/02/13
Previous Clubs: Central Coast Mariners, Belconnen United, ANU FC (on loan at Melbourne Victory while with Celtic)

PROFILES

DAVID TURNBULL

Position: Midfielder   **Squad Number:** 14
D.O.B: 10/07/99   **Born:** Carluke, Scotland
Height: 6'1"   **Signed:** 27/08/20
Debut: v Ross County (a) 5-0, (SPFL) 12/09/20
Previous Clubs: Motherwell

NIR BITTON

Position: Midfielder   **Squad Number:** 6
D.O.B: 30/10/91   **Born:** Ashdod, Israel
Height: 6'5"   **Signed:** 30/08/13
Debut: v AC Milan (a) 0-2, (UCL) 18/09/13
Previous Clubs: FC Ashdod

GIORGOS GIAKOUMAKIS

Position: Striker
D.O.B: 09/12/94   **Born:** Heraklion, Greece
Height: 6'1"   **Signed:** 31/08/21
Debut: n/a*
Previous Clubs: VVV-Venlo, Gornik Zabrze (loan), OFI
(loan), AEK Athens, Episkopi (loan), Platanias, Atsalenios

LIAM SCALES

Position: Defender   **Squad Number:** 5
D.O.B: 08/08/98   **Born:** Barndarrig, Ireland
Height: 6'2"   **Signed:** 27/08/21
Debut: n/a*
Previous Clubs: Shamrock Rovers, UCD,
Arklow Town

*Hadn't made debut at time of going to print.

PARADISE

MIKEY JOHNSTON

Position: Striker   **Squad Number:** 73
D.O.B: 19/04/99   **Born:** Glasgow, Scotland
Height: 5'10"
Debut: v St Johnstone (h) 4-1, (SPFL) 06/05/17
Previous Clubs: Celtic Youth

JOAO FILIPE JOTA

Position: Striker
D.O.B: 30/03/99   **Born:** Lisbon, Portugal
Height: 5'9"   **Signed:** 31/08/21
Debut: n/a*
Previous Clubs: Valladolid (loan), Benfica

LIEL ABADA

Position: Forward   **Squad Number:** 11
D.O.B: 03/10/01   **Born:** Petah Tikva, Israel
Height: 5'5"   **Signed:** 14/07/21
Debut: v FC Midtjylland (h) 1-1, (CL) 20/07/21
Previous Clubs: Maccabi Petah Tikva

KYOGO FURUHASHI

Position: Forward   **Squad Number:** 8
D.O.B: 20/01/95   **Born:** Nara, Japan
Height: 5'7"   **Signed:** 16/07/21
Debut: v Hearts (a) 1-2, (SPFL) 31/07/21
Previous Clubs: Vissel Kobe, FC Gifu

PROFILES

CARL STARFELT

Position: Defender   **Squad Number:** 4
D.O.B: 01/06/95   **Born:** Stockholm, Sweden
Height: 6'1"   **Signed:** 26/07/21
Debut: v Hearts (a) 1-2, (SPFL) 31/07/21
Previous Clubs: Rubin Kazan, IFK Goteborg,
IF Brommapojkarna

ANTHONY RALSTON

Position: Defender   **Squad Number:** 56
D.O.B: 16/11/98   **Born:** Bellshill, Scotland
Height: 5'11"   **Signed:** 16/11/08
Debut: v St Johnstone (a) 1-2, (SPFL) 11/05/16
Previous Clubs: St Johnstone (loan), Dundee Utd (loan)

SCOTT BAIN

Position: Goalkeeper   **Squad Number:** 29
D.O.B: 22/11/91   **Born:** Edinburgh, Scotland
Height: 6'0"   **Signed:** 31/01/18
Debut: v Rangers (a) 3-2, (SPFL) 11/03/18
Previous Clubs: Hibernian (loan), Dundee,
Alloa Athletic, Elgin City (loan), Aberdeen

EWAN HENDERSON

Position: Midfielder   **Squad Number:** 52
D.O.B: 27/03/00   **Born:** Edinburgh, Scotland
Height: 5'9"   **Signed:** 01/08/17
Debut: v Kilmarnock (h) 0-0, (SPFL) 09/05/18
Previous Clubs: Dunfermline (loan), Ross
County (loan)

*Hadn't made debut at time of going to print.

PARADISE

CONOR HAZARD

Position: Goalkeeper **Squad Number:** 65
D.O.B: 05/03/98 **Born:** Downpatrick, Ireland
Height: 6'6" **Signed:** 20/05/14
Debut: v Lille OSC (h) 3-2, (EL), 10/12/20
Previous Clubs: Dundee (loan), Partick Thistle
(loan), Falkirk (loan)

KARAMOKO DEMBELE

Position: Midfielder **Squad Number:** 77
D.O.B: 22/02/03 **Born:** London, England
Height: 5'3"
Debut: v Hearts (h) 2-1, (SPFL) 19/5/19
Previous Clubs: Celtic Youth

CHRISTOPHER JULLIEN

Position: Defender **Squad Number:** 2
D.O.B: 22/03/93 **Born:** Lagny-sur-Marne, France
Height: 6'5" **Signed:** 28/06/19
Debut: v Nomme Kalju (a) 2-0, (UCL) 30/07/19
Previous Clubs: Toulouse, Dijon (loan), SC
Freiburg, Auxerre

OSAZE URHOGHIDE

Position: Defender **Squad Number:** 26
D.O.B: 04/07/00 **Born:** Netherlands
Height: 6'2" **Signed:** 01/07/21
Debut: n/a*
Previous Clubs: Sheffield Wednesday,
AFC Wimbledon

PROFILES

LUCA CONNELL
Position: Midfielder **Squad Number:** 28
D.O.B: 20/04/01 **Born:** Liverpool, England
Height: 5'10" **Signed:** 29/06/19
Debut: n/a*
Previous Clubs: Bolton Wanderers,
Queen's Park (loan)

LIAM SHAW
Position: Midfielder **Squad Number:** 30
D.O.B: 12/03/01 **Born:** Sheffield, England
Height: 6'2" **Signed:** 15/06/21
Debut: n/a*
Previous Clubs: Sheffield Wednesday,
Chesterfield (loan)

BOLI BOLINGOLI-MBOMBO
Position: Defender **Squad Number:** 23
D.O.B: 01/07/95 **Born:** Antwerp, Belgium
Height: 5'11" **Signed:** 03/07/19
Debut: v FK Sarajevo (a) 3-1, (UCL) 9/07/19
Previous Clubs: Rapid Vienna, Sint-Truidense
(loan), Club Brugge, Istanbul Basaksehir (loan)

STEPHEN WELSH
Position: Defender **Squad Number:** 57
D.O.B: 19/01/00 **Born:** Coatbridge, Scotland
Height: 5'9" **Signed:** 01/07/18
Debut: v Hamilton Accies (a) 4-1, (SPFL) 02/02/20
Previous Clubs: Morton (loan)

*Hadn't made debut at time of going to print.

PARADISE

GREG TAYLOR

Position: Defender **Squad Number:** 3
D.O.B: 05/11/97 **Born:** Greenock, Scotland
Height: 5'7" **Signed:** 02/09/19
Debut: v St Mirren (h) 2-0, (SPFL) 30/10/19
Previous Clubs: Kilmarnock

ISMAILA SORO

Position: Midfielder **Squad Number:** 12
D.O.B: 07/05/98 **Born:** Yakasse-Me-Agou, Ivory Coast
Height: 5'7" **Signed:** 27/01/20
Debut: v Ross County (a) 5-0, (SPFL) 12/09/20
Previous Clubs: Bnei Yehuda, Gomel, Saxan

ALBIAN AJETI

Position: Forward **Squad Number:** 10
D.O.B: 26/02/97 **Born:** Basel, Switzerland
Height: 6'0" **Signed:** 13/08/20
Debut: v KR Reykjavik (h) 6-0, (UCL) 18/08/20
Previous Clubs: West Ham, St Gallen, FC Ausburg, Basel

CAMERON CARTER-VICKERS

Position: Defender
D.O.B: 31/12/97 **Born:** Southend-on-Sea, England
Height: 6'0" **Signed:** 31/08/21
Debut: n/a*
Previous Clubs: AFC Bournemouth (loan), Luton Town (loan), Stoke City (loan), Swansea City (loan), Ipswich Town (loan), Sheffield United (loan), Tottenham Hotspur

PROFILES

ADAM MONTGOMERY

Position: Defender   **Squad Number:** 54
D.O.B: 18/07/02   **Born:** Livingston, Scotland
Height: 5' 6"   **Signed:** 01/07/19
Debut: v St Johnstone (h) 4-0, (SPFL) 12/05/21
Previous Clubs: Celtic Youth

JOE HART

Position: Goalkeeper   **Squad Number:** 15
D.O.B: 19/04/87   **Born:** Shrewsbury, England
Height: 6'5"   **Signed:** 03/08/21
Debut: v FK Jablonec (a) 4-2, (EL) 05/08/21
Previous Clubs: Tottenham Hotspur, Burnley, West Ham, Torino (loan), Birmingham City (loan), Blackpool (loan), Tranmere Rovers (loan), Manchester City, Shrewsbury Town

JAMES McCARTHY

Position: Midfielder   **Squad Number:** 16
D.O.B: 12/11/90   **Born:** Glasgow, Scotland
Height: 5'11"   **Signed:** 03/08/21
Debut: v Hearts (h) 3-2, (LC) 15/08/21
Previous Clubs: Hamilton Accies, Wigan Athletic, Everton, Crystal Palace

JOSIP JURANOVIC

Position: Defender   **Squad Number:** 88
D.O.B: 16/08/95   **Born:** Zagreb, Croatia
Height: 5'8"   **Signed:** 21/08/21
Debut: v Rangers (a) 0-1, (SPFL) 29/08/21
Previous Clubs: Legia Warsaw, Hajduk Split, Dubrava

*Hadn't made debut at time of going to print.

A SEASON TO REMEMBER

CELTIC GHIRLS HAVE THEIR MOST SUCCESSFUL CAMPAIGN YET

IT all came down to the final day of the season, and the permutations of what could unfold as Celtic took on Motherwell while Glasgow City hosted Rangers, with both games being broadcast live simultaneously.

City held the ace card, though, as not only had they already qualified for a UEFA Champions League spot, but a win over Rangers would secure them the title.

Their opponents, on the other hand, had to beat City while also hoping that Motherwell would defeat Celtic, meaning that Rangers would leapfrog the Hoops by one point and grab the second Champions League spot.

However, a win for Rangers over Glasgow City, even by 1-0, would also pave the way for anything more than a three-goal win for the Hoops giving Celtic the title on goal difference.

Celtic, meanwhile, just knew that defeating Motherwell in Airdrie would guarantee European football and anything else would be a bonus – they were going for goals aplenty, though, just in case things went their way in the other game at Broadwood.

After the game, the manager said:

"To see the team perform like that, that's what Celtic is all about. It's about heart, passion and fight."

Although, to pin everything on the final day in no way does justice to the magnificent efforts made by the Celts in their first ever fully professional season.

The 8-0 win capped off a remarkable run of form that saw the Ghirls win 12 and draw one of their last 13 fixtures.

They also lost only one goal in their last nine games of a season that saw 14 clean sheets in all - seven each for goalkeepers Chloe Logan and Rachael Johnstone.

The goals were flying in at the other end as well as there were two 10-0 wins, over Hearts and Forfar Farmington and two 8-0 wins, over Forfar Farmington and Motherwell – with 10-0 and 8-0 wins coming in the final two games of the season as it sped to its nail-biting conclusion when goals could really count.

At the end of a breath-taking day, skipper Kelly Clark said:

"People wrote us off so many times and our performances against Glasgow City weren't great but we picked ourselves up after each of those.

"Since that first defeat against them, in the second round of fixtures we've been phenomenal. We were unlucky against Glasgow City but I don't know if Glasgow City expected us to push them all the way to the last day of the season and I'm so proud that we did."

Even more drama was added to an already potent mix when, on the morning of the game, no fewer than **SEVEN** Celts were ruled out due to Covid restrictions.

That had little impact on the game, though, as while City beat Rangers 2-0 in Cumbernauld, Fran Alonso was overwhelmed with pride after his young side defeated Motherwell 8-0 to secure their dream of playing in Europe's most prestigious club competition.

FIRST CLASS STAMP OF EXCELLENCE

LANDMARK SEASON FOR CHLOE CRAIG

AMONG the many highlights of 2021 for Hoops defender and former postal worker, Chloe Craig, there was the personal accolade of her 200th game in the green and white of Celtic – the only senior club she has ever been involved with.

Since turning professional at the start of the season, the No.6 posted her intentions early and the year produced a sackful of memories as she has really pushed the envelope by delivering on all fronts for Celtic since then.

It was on May 16 as the season geared up for a thrilling climax, that Celtic travelled to the Oriam to take on Hearts and not only did the Celts claim a 3-0 win, Craig marked the occasion of her 200th game by scoring the opener – her 65th goal for the club.

2010 **2021**

Craig didn't stop at 200 games and 65 goals, though, as she finished the season with her 205th game, scoring her 68th goal – an average of a goal every three games is an astounding achievement for a defender.

She said after the milestone match: *"It was the perfect moment for a perfect occasion I guess. It's surreal to think I've had 200 appearances and to cap it off with a goal - there's no better feeling."*

When she arrived at the club 13 years ago as a teenager, making her 200th appearance couldn't have been further from her mind as she could barely believe she would be training among players she had looked up to.

The vice-captain recalled: *"I never even thought it would be possible to get an appearance for the first team. You used to turn up to training and you'd see these idols like Rhonda Jones, Suzanne Grant and Jen Beattie that were training next to you.*

"So to even get that chance to step up into the first team was a dream come true, but 200 appearances later, it's just so surreal. It's a privilege to me and my family to be able to walk on to the park knowing that."

SPOT THE DIFFERENCE

THERE are 10 differences between these two photographs of Mariah Lee celebrating her goal against Rangers at Celtic Park. The first one has been circled, but can you spot the rest?

WHO AM I?

ONE

1. I was with Hibernian before joining Celtic, but I never played for them.
2. I was born in Edinburgh but started with Aberdeen.
3. I made my international debut for Scotland against Mexico.

TWO

1. I have an Under-20 World Cup-winning medal.
2. As well as playing in my home country, I have also played in Germany.
3. I scored a cup-winning goal for Celtic.

THREE

1. I travelled to South America to make my international debut.
2. I was 17 years old when I made my debut in senior football.
3. I made my Celtic debut in Italy.

FOUR

1. In Season 2018/19, I played more minutes than any other player in world football.
2. I have captained my country as well as Celtic.
3. I scored in successive games against Rangers just six days apart.

THE CELTIC MAZE

STEPHEN Welsh was training at Barrowfield with his Celtic Academy team-mates last season when he got the call to report to Lennoxtown to try out with the first team. Can you help him get from one Celtic training camp to the other?

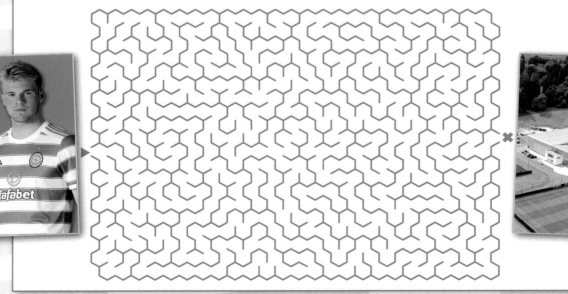

Find out if you're right on page 62/63.

47

THE GREEN AND WHITEWASH
CELTIC WOMEN PAVE WAY TO UEFA CHAMPIONS LEAGUE DEBUT WITH A GLASGOW DERBY TREBLE

A MAJOR, indeed crucial, part of Celtic Women's history-making UEFA Champions League qualification for the first time ever was three vital wins over Rangers during the SWPL schedule.

Hard-fought victories of two 1-0 wins followed by a 2-1 clincher were among the many highlights of a season that delivered so much for the Ghirls.

The last of those wins, thanks to goals from Kelly Clark and Sarah Ewens put Fran Alonso's side second in the table, just three points behind Glasgow City with three games remaining as the three Glaswegian sides fought out a tri-way battle for the title and/or European football.

It was a win that had the manager gasping:

"It was totally deserved, and I'm running out of words to describe how proud I feel about the fighting spirit and the passion they show on the football pitch wearing the Celtic top."

Ewens' goal at Rangers' Training Ground on May 23 came just seven minutes from the end after the home side had equalised Clark's opener.

The first game at the same venue, though, the previous November was even more dramatic as the sides were in the 92nd minute when Jodie Bartle looked to have scored an amazing last-gasp winner.

Incredibly, though, as the joyous Ghirls celebrated, the referee pointed to the spot, cancelling the 'goal' and awarding the Hoops a penalty.

Summer Green held her nerve, though, and buried the spot-kick for the opening derby victory and a vital three points.

Possibly the pick of the bunch, though, was when the Ghirls grasped the opportunity to take to the hallowed turf of Paradise on April 21 and play against their rivals under the lights at Celtic Park.

And Mariah Lee couldn't have chosen a better time to score her first Celtic goal when she calmly slotted away the winner in a crucial 1-0 win for the Ghirls.

The delighted scorer said:

"Against Rangers, just being in Celtic Park and playing there was awesome, I just wanted to capitalise on that opportunity.

"And to get a win! It was 0-0 and we were gunning to beat Rangers, so scoring, putting the team up and just everything coming together made it an unbelievable first goal for Celtic."

QUADRUPLE QUALITY

THE SCOTTISH CUP FINAL THAT CREATED HISTORY

THIS wasn't just any old Scottish Cup final, if there indeed could be such a thing. For a start, Covid and the Lockdown ensured the game was held back from 2019/20, and played in 2020/21, although it still went ahead during the 2020 calendar year just a few days before Christmas.

Also due to the pandemic, there were no supporters inside Hampden as Celtic and Hearts met for the second year running in the final.

Celtic were also going for their 40th win and, if they managed that, they would create a big piece of history thanks to their 2-1 final win the previous year.

That win delivered a third consecutive Scottish Cup victory as the Hoops joined Queen's Park (twice), Vale of Leven, Rangers (three times) and Aberdeen as three-in-a-row winners – but no club had ever won four-in-a-row.

The fourth successive win looked on as Celtic took a 2-0 lead, only for Hearts to claw it back to 2-2. The Hoops took the lead again in extra-time, only for Hearts to equalise once more to take the game to a penalty cliffhanger.

This was only the third time in Scottish Cup history that the final had gone to penalties – and the omens didn't look good for Celtic as they lost 9-8 on spot-kicks to Aberdeen in 1990, while Hearts defeated Gretna 4-2 in the other penalty shoot-out in 2006.

In a nail-biting scenario designed for heroes, two stood out from the many – young Irishman, Conor Hazard in the Celtic goal saved two of the spot-kicks, meaning that the Hampden spotlight fell on Kristoffer Ajer for the last of the 10 penalties.

The Norwegian belted the ball right down the middle and history was made once more.

The 2020 Scottish Cup final was remarkable for so many reasons – not least of all being that it clinched the historic Quadruple Treble for Celtic.

MATCH FACTS

2019/20 Scottish Cup final
Hampden Park, Glasgow
December 20, 2020

CELTIC...3
(Christie 18, Edouard 29, Griffiths 105)

HEARTS...3
(Boyce 48, Kingsley 68, Ginnelly 111)

Celtic won 4-3 on penalties

FORREST FLASHBACK FILES No.3

JAMES FORREST'S LIFE AS A CELT

IN our final look back at some of James Forrest's Celtic Annual appearances we visit 2015 when, in Players' Past Pastimes, he let us know about his early days as an ace on the tennis court.

...ndball at
...Iceland.

James Forrest

I played tennis. You know what it's like growing up, you will play any sport that is going so I played a bit of that. There were tennis courts around the corner from where I lived and that is why I played it a lot. I was okay but then I got to around 14/15 and decided to stop playing and concentrate on football. My best shot? I was an all-rounder. I haven't played it in a couple of years now.

JAMES FORREST

1st

First goal

I can remember scoring my first goal for Celtic when I was in the under-10s. It was at Barrowfield and it was the first proper game that we played. We were playing 11-a-side but was from 18-yard box to 18-yard box. It was just a really good strike and I have never forgotten it. I was buzzing at the time.

1st

First strip

I can't remember the first one, but I always had about six or seven tops for English and Spanish teams. I had Man United tops and I remember having a Chelsea one. I also had Barca, Real Madrid strips, and even one from Atletico Madrid at one point.

1st

First silverware

At the end of every year, Celtic always used to go on trips abroad and it was good to play against foreign teams. I remember getting to the final one year and we also got to the final of the Villarreal tournament when I was with the U19s. My first winner's medal would have been in the Glasgow Cup in 2008 when I was playing for the U17s. I must have been about 15 or 16 and we beat Rangers 3-1 in Airdrie and I scored.

We come more up to date when due to Lockdown, it was Trophy On Tour as far as the SPFL silverware was concerned when the 'presentation' consisted of the trophy doing the rounds of the players' houses.

SKIPPER WORDSEARCH

HIDDEN in this word grid are the past 20 Celtic captains – and that stretches back quite far, so see how many you can find.

You might want to get your parents or even grandparents involved in this game as well!

```
C A L L U M M C G R E G O R I P T N E N E F
E A O Y C I F D E P Q J J N I L O I Z A U S
S A I D G G N W P A K O O R O N X D G A U Q
I U T L G M I N A U B H C R I U Y H O M O N
N H N R E M A E N L N N K F I T A I J K O P
R Q R A Y B R I N M Y M S Q F U O C X U S E
K O E C M M G L A C Y C T E C N H M R K C F
L T E E L C C L X S J P E P L J J C B C Q T
K V R R A W M E F T N H I U A A Z U F O L A
T E S E D U Y N E A D A N Y C O L O Y C Y K
N Y N Y B S N N E Y T I V K U L Y A M A O D
S O U N N M N O P H D L I E I W K V D E O N
C B L P Y Q A N K A P E R E Y C Y E O P P O
O O F L R D D L C Q M E N O A B E I N E N Y
T B A G A C A O L C A C T M Y T B P K I F L
T B B N F F G L N U M R Y S X A I O R T U E
B Y A Z P Z N A G Y A K M S A M I V B R A I
R H N I T B M A L L N P I T J P W T O E R L
O O Z C A A M L E U I D H N M N N R K B F L
W G O Y R C I G D S E S F I E Z M T I E F I
N G Y A O B R F T E E H I W Y C K E N N W
```

CALLUM MCGREGOR   PAUL LAMBERT   KENNY DALGLISH   JOCK STEIN

SCOTT BROWN   TOM BOYD   BILLY MCNEILL   SEAN FALLON

STEPHEN MCMANUS   PAUL MCSTAY   DUNKY MACKAY   JOHN MCPHAIL

NEIL LENNON   ROY AITKEN   BERTIE PEACOCK   WILLIE LYON

JACKIE MCNAMARA   DANNY MCGRAIN   BOBBY EVANS   BOBBY HOGG

DEBUT DESTINATION

THESE eight Celts all made their debuts for the club at different grounds around Scotland and Europe – but can you pair up each player with the venue where they took their bow?

Callum McGregor

James Forrest

Nir Bitton

Tom Rogic

Joe Hart

Christopher Jullien

Stephen Welsh

David Turnbull

Lillekula Arena, Tallin

Stadion Strelnice, Jablonec

New Douglas Park, Hamilton

KR-vollur, Reykjavik

San Siro, Milan

Victoria Park, Dingwall

Celtic Park, Glasgow

Caledonian Stadium, Inverness

HELLO, GOODBYE

THE transfer window sees players come and go all over the world, but can you tell us which Celtic players arrived from the clubs on the left before moving to the clubs on the right?

Arrived from	Moved to	Player
1. Hibernian	Aberdeen	
2. Feyenoord	Barcelona	
3. Borussia Dortmund	Livingston	
4. Aston Villa	Preston North End	
5. Cardiff City	Crystal Palace	

Find out if you're right on page 62/63.

LEGENDS BC
(BEFORE CELTIC)

A look at four Celtic stars of the past and the career path that took them to Paradise – and the stats they created in the green and white Hoops.

HENRIK LARSSON

Henrik Larsson began his football career in 1988 at the age of 17 when he signed for Swedish team Hogaborg BK. After four years there, he then moved to Helsingborg, where he displayed his talent, scoring 50 goals in 56 appearances. It was an impressive return in just over a year, and it wasn't long before Dutch club Feyenoord came calling and he moved to The Netherlands in 1993. It took him a while to settle into his new environment, though his scoring record continued to rise over the course of the next four years. However, in 1997 he indicated to the club that he wanted to leave. Celtic, now managed by Wim Jansen, who had been technical director at Feyenoord when they signed the player, moved to buy him and after a protracted legal wrangle, he moved to Paradise in July 1997 for what would prove to be a bargain fee of £650,000.

CELTIC CAREER APPEARANCES

	A	S	G
League	218	3	174
League Cup	11	-	10
Scottish Cup	25	-	23
Europe	58	-	35
Total	315	3	242

CELTIC CAREER MAJOR HONOURS: 8
LEAGUE: 4, SCOTTISH CUP: 2, LEAGUE CUP: 2

TOMMY BURNS

Tommy Burns had a rather short road to Paradise as he lived not far along the road in the Calton and the draw of Celtic Park would pull him and his mates away from honing their skills in Soho Street. He featured for St Mungo's Academy as well as St Mary's Boys' Guild and the famed nursery side, Eastercraigs before signing an S-form with Celtic in 1970. He signed professionally in 1973 and was farmed out to Maryhill Juniors before making his first-team debut in the Hoops. And, of course, after giving up the playing side, TB returned to his spiritual home as manager.

CELTIC CAREER APPEARANCES

	A	S	G
League	324	32	52
League Cup	70	-	15
Scottish Cup	38	5	12
Europe	31	3	3
Total	463	40	82

CELTIC CAREER MAJOR HONOURS: 11
LEAGUE: 6, SCOTTISH CUP: 4, LEAGUE CUP: 1

JACKIE McNAMARA

Jackie McNamara joined Dunfermline Athletic's youth set-up as a 17-year-old in September 1991, and he made his first-team debut the following year against Arbroath. On Bert Paton's appointment in 1993, he became the regular right-back at East End Park and was soon causing a stir with his performances. Adventurous, skilful and comfortable in possession, McNamara emerged as a potent attacking weapon for the Pars as they narrowly missed out on promotion from the First Division. The Fifers endured a similar scenario the following season as Aberdeen defeated them in a play-off, but McNamara, who had already been capped eight times for Scotland Under-21s, was always going to be destined for a career at the top and his departure was close at hand.

CELTIC CAREER APPEARANCES			
	A	S	G
League	221	36	10
League Cup	17	2	1
Scottish Cup	26	5	3
Europe	43	9	1
Total	307	52	15

CELTIC CAREER MAJOR HONOURS: 10
LEAGUE: 4, SCOTTISH CUP: 3, LEAGUE CUP: 3

TOM BOYD

Tom Boyd grew up in the industrial heart of Lanarkshire and quickly his steely determination transferred to the football field as his talent as a defender took him into a career as a professional footballer. His career would start at his local side Motherwell where he quickly became a fans' favourite as a commanding presence at the back who also had the skill to move forward. This was showcased when he captained the side to victory against Dundee United in the 1991 Scottish Cup final, widely regarded as one of the most entertaining. His performances during his eight years at Motherwell saw him attract the attention of Chelsea, and with a Scottish Cup winner's medal in his pocket, he headed off to London. After a year at Stamford Bridge, the call came from his Bhoyhood heroes and, with Tony Cascarino heading in the opposite direction in a swap deal, Tom Boyd made his way to Paradise.

CELTIC CAREER APPEARANCES			
	A	S	G
League	296	10	2
League Cup	31	2	-
Scottish Cup	31	3	-
Europe	33	1	-
Total	391	16	2

CELTIC CAREER MAJOR HONOURS: 8
LEAGUE: 3, SCOTTISH CUP: 2, LEAGUE CUP: 3

SCOTT BROWN AND CELTIC'S 600+ CLUB

WHEN on April 14, 1925 the great Alec McNair played his 641st and last Celtic game at the grand old age of 41 years, three months and 25 days old, surely no-one at the time thought that tally would ever be neared never mind surpassed.

After all, his Celtic first-team career had lasted all but 21 years, and that was astounding longevity even back then.

However, the eventual introduction of the League Cup followed by European football opened up other avenues of game-time – but avenues that only successful players in successful teams could take advantage of fully.

So McNair's record stood until the 1970s when Billy McNeill overtook him, and since then, Danny McGrain, Roy Aitken, Pat Bonner and Paul McStay have also joined Celtic's 600+ Club – Hoops legends one and all, and players who came through the ranks at the club.

Even so, after the mid-1990s when Bonner and McStay had been the latest to join the Celtic 600+ Club ranks, the idea of anyone else gaining admittance to the club seemed far-fetched. After all, the two main criteria were being a mainstay of a team that regularly fought all the way to finals of competitions **AND** staying with the club well over 10 years – something that is increasingly irregular in modern-day football.